SO, WHAT CAN I EAT NOW?!

LIVING WITHOUT DAIRY, SOY, EGGS, AND WHEAT

[HEALTHY SUNDAY DINNER EDITION]

An excerpt from the original cookbook.

BASIC RECIPES TO JUMPSTART A HEALTHY LIFESTYLE LOW FAT • LOW CALORIES • LOW SUGAR • LOW SODIUM

Rhonda Peters

Book Division of Rhonda's Cooking, LLC

D1205566

Note: This book is intended only as an informative guide for those wishing to know more about health issues. Readers are advised to consult a health care provider before making any changes in their diet. The reader assumes all responsibility for the consequences of any actions taken based on the information presented in this book. The information in this book is based on the author's research and experience. Every attempt has been made to ensure that the information is accurate; however, the author cannot accept liability for any errors that may exist. The facts and theories on diet, inflammation, and health are subject to interpretation, and the conclusions and recommendations presented here may not agree with other interpretations.

Amazon Version - Second Edition - 1.1.1 - Build 2021
Original Source: So, What Can I Eat Now?!
Created by: Rhonda's Cooking, LLC
Published by: Rhonda's Cooking, LLC

Rhonda's Cooking, LLC
PO Box 153
Laveen, AZ 85339

Chief Creative Director: Clemille Peters, Jr.
Interior Layout and Design: Clemille Peters, Jr. and Krause Creative
Cover Design: Krause Creative
Photography: Chris Marchetti Photography
Food Stylists: Emily Bolton and Rhonda Peters
Assistant Food Stylists: Chris Marchetti and Dave Branstrator
Copyediting: Glory Davis, Susan Coartney, and Lubertha Peters

Library of Congress Cataloging-in-Publication Data

Peters, Rhonda.
So, What Can I Eat Now?!

Library of Congress Control Number: 2009924889

To order a paperback or hardback copy of this original cookbook visit Blurb.com.

To order the ebook versions of the original version, please visit Amazon.com to download on any device.

Developed and Designed in the United States of America

Contents

Acknowledgements

There were so many friends, family members, and acquaintances that supported and encouraged me in a variety of ways as I wrote So What Can I Eat Now. I would like to take this opportunity to thank each of them.

The highest praise and thanks go to God for giving me the inspiration and endurance to write this book. I am grateful that He has given me an opportunity and a platform to share my experiences and to inspire people with various health challenges to eat a nutritious, life-supporting diet.

Sincere thanks to my wonderful mother and friend, Lubertha Peters, an awesome cook whom I credit for teaching me the fundamentals and techniques of cooking. When I struggled with the last phase of writing this project, my mom was a very encouraging recipe editor and tester who motivated me whenever I felt like quitting. Thanks also to my dad, Clemille Peters, Sr. for supporting and encouraging me daily, for showing interest in the cookbook and for promoting it to his co-workers and acquaintances. I value my parent's devotion and want them to know that it was indeed a blessing to finish writing my book in the home where I first learned to cook—at home in Angie, Louisiana.

Words cannot express my gratefulness to my brother, Clemille Peters, Jr., for his major contribution as chief creative director and graphic designer. From the front cover to the back, he has done a phenomenal job. As coach, encourager, and supporter throughout this journey, he was always there to listen to me as I brainstormed even though he was busy with launching Konsole Kingz, LLC.

Heartfelt appreciation goes to Pastors Sean Moore and Erica Moore for being my first recipe testers. Special appreciation to Pastor Erica for being open-minded and willing to test my concept recipes. I am also thankful for her clever and constructive feedback.

Thanks to Mrs. Emily Bolton for being my sous-chef and food stylist during the photo shoot. I could not have survived without her that day! Thanks to Chris Marchetti and Dave of Marchetti Photography for being compassionate and willing to help even if it meant being a food stylist! I am also appreciative to Carrie Hernandez for taking care of me at the end of the photo shoot.

Sincere thanks to Kurt Krause of Krause Creative. Kurt's commitment, professionalism and design experience were instrumental to this book. He stepped in and delivered an impressive cover design and brought closure to this project.

Thanks to the best nationally certified English teacher of all-time, Glory Davis, my former high school English teacher. At the last minute, Ms. Davis rearranged her schedule to assist me with editing parts of this book. Thanks for always being available.

Finally, I acknowledge the following people who, in one way or the other, were instrumental in making this book a success: Dr. Victor and Catherine Eagan, Kimberly Dellafosse, Patricia Fuller, Gerry Gonzales, Shavon Griffin, Monique Hayward, Kesha Hodge, Pastor Sidney Jones and Mrs. Jones, Tammye Keegan, Paulette Laster, Dr. Leon, Justine Lopez, Leah Martin, Stephanie Monarch, Christian Mordh, Elaine Cauley, Sherry Moss, Antoinette Peters, Emma Ross, Nefertari Thomas, Daniel and Kendra Tillman, Tretessa Johnson, Stephanie Sinclair, Marie-Eve Thomas, and Wealthy Women Club Members.

Foreword

There are many books available to the public in the fields of nutrition and alternative medicine. It is difficult for the public to sift through the varying opinions of how we should eat. As a Naturopathic Physician of 16 years I have seen how difficult it can be for patients to know how to eat. Or they have great knowledge of balanced eating but are frustrated by their lack of sufficient results.

In this thought then, it is often a personal experience which makes the greatest impact upon us. In presenting this nutritional information, Rhonda not only utilizes her years of cooking experience but brings into her work the disciplines of methodical scientific analysis.

I have seen in her as well as with many patients the impact of foods on health and in the function or dysfunction of the body. Many do not realize that the foods which they are consuming are adding to their health complaints. Naturopathic Medicine takes the position that indeed we are what we eat and seeks to identify in every individual their unique nutritional requirements.

A strong example of this is the fact that while the grains provide nutrients and fulfillment in the dining experience, some cannot tolerate the gluten components within them. And so what would normally be a healthy and reasonable recommendation for one may not work for another.

The world of cooking and nutrition are wrought with traditions sometimes not based on true understandings of the science of the human body. Rhonda offers her unbiased perspective on the challenges of educating the public about their food options.

Her knowledge of mathematics and physics and their application to food preparation makes this book not only unique but also extremely helpful.

Rhonda's work will no doubt be a great service to humanity furthering our knowledge of nutrition and cooking.

Therefore I am profoundly pleased and honored to recommend her book to anyone who would be bold enough to "go outside the box" in exploring their eating options.

Dr. Gilberto Leon NMD

About the Author

Rhonda is a Diet Counselor and Certified Professional Food Manager with over 10 years of engineering and business experience in the high-technology industry. She has coached a number of clients and taught them about healthier food alternatives in order to help them feel great physically and mentally. Since learning about her intolerance to dairy, soy and eggs, Rhonda has been on a quest to convert the traditional southern meals that she grew up eating in Louisiana to accommodate her new diet.

Through extensive research and testing, Rhonda has developed a number of healthy breakfast foods, appetizers, entrees and desserts that can offer people alternative, delicious meals that are healthy with excellent flavors.

Rhonda has been a member of The Food Allergy and Anaphylaxis Network (FAAN), Celiac Disease Foundation, American Heart Association, and American Diabetes Association.

Introduction

I grew up in a small town called Angie, which is about 100 miles north of New Orleans, Louisiana. With a population of less than 5000, Angie is a place where basically everyone knows everyone. When I was growing up, there was no McDonald's, Boston Market, or Popeye's in my neck of the woods. Consequently, we had home cooked meals everyday; there were no days off in our kitchen! Everyday my mother made certain that we had a good hot breakfast and a full course meal for dinner!

Seafood Gumbo, fried catfish and hush puppies, smothered pork chops with rice and gravy, chicken and dumplings, greens and cornbread cooked with smoked ham hocks, peach cobbler, red velvet cake, and the list goes on. These are just a few of the wonderful dishes that my mother made that were typical of Angie and other Southern towns. Yes, my mother was an excellent cook, and everyone bragged on her chili, gumbo, and pecan pie.

With a mother like that, it was inevitable that I would follow her footsteps. I have been cooking since the age of 9, starting with my award winning, blue ribbon Southern pecan pie. Later I moved to other traditional Southern dishes such as fried chicken, cornbread dressing, red beans & rice, and collard greens. By age 12, I had learned to cut a whole chicken into its eight main parts. And I had mastered the art of momma's secret seasoning.

When I graduated from college and moved into my own apartment, I really put my skills to use. I cooked daily. I loved getting into the kitchen to create—it was therapeutic! It was so exciting to taste the food and give it the "just like mom's" stamp of approval. As years passed, I gained knowledge about other types of cuisines such as Italian and Chinese and later learned to cook some of those recipes. Even though these recipes where good, I would still infuse my Louisiana spices into each dish. For, I enjoyed eating these rich, spicy, salty and sugary foods typical of my area.

THE CHANGE...

When I was twenty-three years old, my health changed drastically. I had problems with my thyroid gland and joints in my hands. After seeing a number of doctors and specialists, I learned that I had hyperthyroidism and rheumatoid arthritis. I was in shock! Then, I knew nothing of a thyroid, and as for arthritis, I thought that was an old folk's disease. After all, that's what my grandma had. So, what did all of this mean for me? Well, for years it meant a physical and emotional, "yo-yo" lifestyle where things would go from one extreme to the next in a very short time. Because my immune system was dysfunctional, my body literally worked against me. My weight fluctuated and my vision weakened. My hands swelled so much that I could not grip a toothbrush, zip my clothes, or drive.

I tried many new drugs to help me feel better. For the hyperthyroidism, I took various doses of synthyroid, as well as the radioactive iodine treatment. The radioactive iodine cured the hyperthyroidism, but over time left me with hypothyroidism. For the treatment for the arthritis, let's just say that whenever the FDA approved a new drug for arthritis, my doctor introduced it to me and I was sure to test it out. Two of the many drugs that I used to help me relieve the pain of the rheumatoid arthritis were VIOXX® and Celebrex. Unfortunately, neither of these helped me on a long term basis. Overtime I accepted the fact that I would have "flare-ups" of inflammation in my wrists twice a year from arthritis. In a like manner, I expected the excessive weight gain due to thyroid imbalance. After seven years of pain and frustration, I met Dr. Don Colbert, Director of The Divine Health Wellness Center, who introduced me to naturopathic medicine. He expressed the importance of living a healthy life by making a few adjustments to reduce stress and to eat healthier. I purchased two of Dr. Colbert's books, one on arthritis and the other on thyroid disease. After reading those two books, I learned many new things about autoimmune diseases. At that point, I decided to consult with a naturopathic physician.

THE REVELATION

Based on a saliva test administered by my naturopathic doctor, I learned that I had intolerances to dairy (specifically to the casein, a milk protein), soy and eggs. I was in shock and heartbroken because I knew that I could no longer eat the down-home southern foods that I loved so well. My first thoughts were how I am going to bake cakes and pies? What about my café latte and cappuccino? After learning about my intolerances, I decided to begin a new journey in life, one that would take me far away from my days as a little girl in Angie, Louisiana, one that would free me from the pain and frustration of my thyroid and arthritis diseases—a life free of dairy, soy and eggs.

WHERE DO I GO FROM HERE?

After thirty-two years of Louisiana soul food, where do I go from here? Considering the fact that I have a Bachelor's Degree in Physics and a Master's in Electrical Engineering, I had lots of experience in solving problems through research, so I embraced my new challenge scientifically. My first step was to start with the basics. I went back to all of my recipes, especially my favorites and then began to study the purpose of each ingredient in them. I prioritized the importance of each of my favorite dishes and then started the study with desserts, which happens to be one of my most favorite things to eat. I had no idea how I would re-create the desserts I grew up eating and make them taste good without dairy and egg.

I sought the answer in cookbooks that I collected over the years. The biggest thing that stood out the most was that majority of them did not accommodate my new diet. So, I found myself researching magazines, health journals and the Internet to see how I could cook without dairy, soy or eggs. The more I researched, the more I learned that there have been many books and studies published that analyzes the direct impact of dairy, soy and eggs on rheumatoid arthritis and thyroid disease, as well as other diseases. However, none of these cookbooks had recipes that addressed all three of my intolerances simultaneously. Frustrated, disgusted I threw up my hands and screamed, "So, What Can I Eat Now?!" I knew that I had to create my own book.

THE PURPOSE OF THIS BOOK

My purpose is to give people challenged with weight fluctuations, food allergies/intolerances, autoimmune diseases, and heart diseases hope. I want them to know that they are not alone, that they can enjoy food even if they are burdened with these potentially life threatening illnesses! Specifically, the purpose of this book is as follows:

1. To develop recipes that are 100% free of the three most common allergens, dairy, soy and eggs.

2. To provide recipes that are low in sodium, sugar, fat, and calories that are an excellent diet for people with diabetes, high cholesterol and high blood pressure.

3. To devise healthy and tasteful recipes that minimize complications with diseases such as arthritis and hypo/hyperthyroidism.

4. To create gluten-free recipes for people who are gluten intolerant.

5. Lastly, to empower and teach all people how to cook healthy foods that taste delicious.

Decoding the Nutrition Facts

The nutrition facts for each recipe in this cookbook were calculated based on an average daily 2000 calorie American diet using the Food Processor SQL Software by Esha Research, Inc. Readers are advised to consult a health care provider before making any dietary changes.

CALORIES
Calories are units of energy and refer to the amount of energy in food and the amount of energy the body uses. Carbohydrates, fats and proteins are sources of calories found in food, whereas vitamins, minerals, cholesterol and fiber do not. In this example, 2000 calories are required, and this recipe only makes up 257 calories of the total amount required.

CHOLESTEROL
Cholesterol is a substance found in foods of animal origin and in every body cell. It is recommended that a person in good health consume no more than 300mg of cholesterol per day. However, if a person is at risk of heart disease, then he/she should consume less than 200mg of cholesterol daily.

SODIUM
Sodium is one of the major trace minerals with important properties in its natural state that the body utilizes. This example recipe only has 480mg of sodium, which is less than the 2400mg daily recommended value. However, consume less than 1800mg of sodium daily if diagnosed with hypertension. (Note: 1 teaspoon salt = 2400mg sodium!)

NUTRITION FACTS
Based on a 2000 calorie diet per day

Nutrient	Recipe	Daily
Calories (kcal)	257	2000
Fat (g)	13	65
Saturated Fat (g)	1.2	20
Trans Fat (g)	0	
Poly Unsat Fat (g)	0.2	
Mono Unsat Fat (g)	1.9	
Cholesterol (mg)	0	300
Sodium (mg)	480	2400
Carbohydrates (g)	33	300
Dietary Fiber (g)	8	25
Total Sugars (g)	15	
Protein (g)	6	50
Vitamin A (IU)	52	5000
Vitamin C (mg)	7	60
Calcium (mg)	24	1000
Iron (mg)	5	18

Recipe Nutrition Per Serving

Daily Recommended Nutrition

FAT
Fats supply energy and many body processes. They consist of both saturated and unsaturated fats. Strive for low saturated fats and little to none trans fat (<0.1); select foods high in unsaturated fats. The total amount of fat recommended in this example is 65g, and the recipe has only 13g of fat.

CARBOHYDRATES (ALSO KNOWN AS CARBS)
Carbohydrates are made up of sugars, starches, and fibers. Sugar and starches are the body's main source of energy. Consumption amount depends on one's total calorie need; in this example, based on a 2000 calorie diet, 300g of carbohydrates are recommended, but this recipe only contains 33g.

VITAMINS AND MINERALS
Vitamins and minerals regulate several processes in the body that produce energy and more. In fact, they are important in every process that occurs in the body! This label shows that 5000IUs of Vitamin A are recommended based upon a 2000 calorie diet, but this recipe only contains 52IUs.

NUTRITION FACTS (PER SERVING)
The nutrition facts label indicates the total amount of nutrition per serving for this recipe (gray boxes) in comparison to the standard daily 2000 calorie diet for an adult in the USA (black boxes).

PROTEIN
Proteins build, repair and maintain all of the body tissues. They are the body's other source of energy, when carbohydrates are in short supply. Consumption amount depends on one's body weight; in this example, based on a 2000 calorie diet, 50g of protein are recommended, but this recipe only contains 6g.

RECIPES

Oven-Fried Chicken Wings

Total Servings: 8
Serving Size: 1 wing

In my house, we ate fried chicken almost everyday! This recipe was created to satisfy my cravings for fried chicken, but without actually frying the chicken. Savory, juicy, crispy and golden brown best describe this chicken recipe. It is considered as the best alternative to the infamous fried chicken! This oven-baked delight has the appearance of fried chicken with less fat. Both kids and adults love these wings!

8 whole chicken wings (about 1½ pounds), rinsed and cleaned (remove hair)

½ cup brown rice flour

½ cup quinoa flour

1 teaspoon guar gum

2 teaspoons garlic powder

1 tablespoon onion powder

¼ teaspoon Celtic Sea Salt® Brand

⅛ teaspoon nutmeg

⅛ teaspoon ground white pepper

¼ teaspoon ground sage

¼ teaspoon plus ⅛ teaspoon paprika

2 tablespoons olive oil

1 Preheat the oven to 350°F. Add brown rice flour, quinoa flour, and guar gum to a plastic storage bag. Grease the rack of a roasting pan with 1 tablespoon of the olive oil using a basting brush (or use a baking sheet with a greased cooling rack placed on top of the pan; this will allow the chicken drippings to fall to bottom of pan.) Line the bottom with aluminum foil for easy clean-up.

2 Fold the chicken wing tip underneath the drum portion (the biggest part of the wing); this will form a triangle shape. Mix chicken, garlic powder, onion powder, sea salt, nutmeg, white pepper, sage and paprika in a large bowl by hand until all pieces have been coated with the seasoning. Rinse hands immediately in warm, soapy water to avoid cross contamination.

3 Place 3 or 4 seasoned wings into the storage bag that contains the flour mixture; seal and shake the bag to coat each wing with the flour. Remove wings from the bag, shake off the excess flour, and place onto the greased roasting pan; continue until all wings have been coated with flour. Baste wings with the remaining tablespoon of olive oil using a basting brush and bake for 1 hour. Turn the wings with tongs and bake on the other side, until crispy, about 10 to 15 minutes. Turn the wings once more and bake, until crispy, golden brown, about 10 to 15 minutes.

Tidbit

This recipe can be used with other chicken parts (breast, legs and thighs). However, to reduce the amount of fat and calories, remove the skin first. Try this recipe with skinless thighs; this will be a 50% reduction in calories, fat and sodium in comparison to one chicken wing.

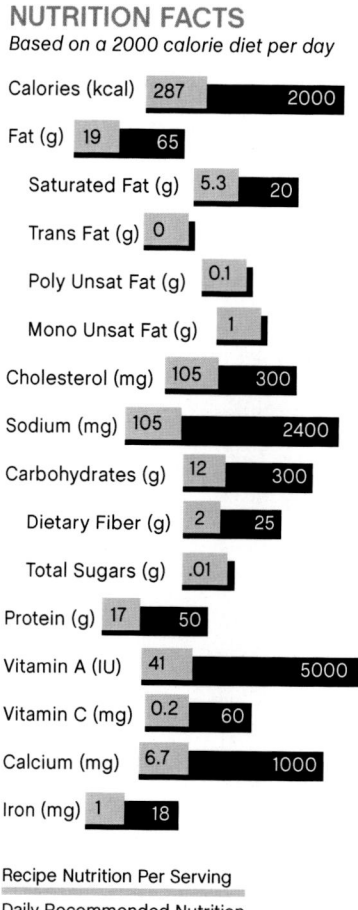

NUTRITION FACTS
Based on a 2000 calorie diet per day

	Recipe Nutrition Per Serving	Daily Recommended Nutrition
Calories (kcal)	287	2000
Fat (g)	19	65
Saturated Fat (g)	5.3	20
Trans Fat (g)	0	
Poly Unsat Fat (g)	0.1	
Mono Unsat Fat (g)	1	
Cholesterol (mg)	105	300
Sodium (mg)	105	2400
Carbohydrates (g)	12	300
Dietary Fiber (g)	2	25
Total Sugars (g)	.01	
Protein (g)	17	50
Vitamin A (IU)	41	5000
Vitamin C (mg)	0.2	60
Calcium (mg)	6.7	1000
Iron (mg)	1	18

Recipe Nutrition Per Serving

Daily Recommended Nutrition

Southern Style Cabbage

Total Servings: 5
Serving Size: 1 cup

I have very fond memories of eating cabbage mixed with crumbled pieces of cornbread. Green cabbage is one my favorite leafy green vegetables not only because of its taste, but also because it is very easy to prepare and quick to cook! After many tests, I have finally developed a recipe that has very similar flavors as traditional southern cabbage recipes, but without using smoked ham hocks and lard!

1 small green cabbage (about 2 pounds), rinsed

½ cup water

⅛ cup extra-virgin olive oil

2 teaspoons onion powder

¾ teaspoon Celtic Sea Salt® Brand

Pinch ground black pepper

1. Remove the outer leaves of the cabbage and cut into 8 quarters. Remove the core and cut cabbage into ½-inch wide strips.

2. Bring water to a boil in a small stockpot and add cabbage strips, oil, onion powder, salt and pepper. Reduce heat to medium and cook, covered, stirring often, about 15 to 20 minutes, or until desired tenderness. Be sure to pay attention to the cabbage to avoid scorching. Remove pot from the heat when done.

Tidbits

Cabbage can be prepared in a number of ways. However, the traditional Southern style cabbage is boiled with smoked meat and cooked until very soft. If desired, simply add ½ cup chopped smoked turkey leg and an additional cup of water to this recipe. Boil meat for about 30 minutes before adding cabbage. Typically smoked meat has lots of sodium, so if you have blood pressure issues, you will need to adjust the salt accordingly.

If you like the core, do not discard. Simply dice it into bite-size pieces and cook with the cabbage leaves.

NUTRITION FACTS
Based on a 2000 calorie diet per day

	Recipe Nutrition Per Serving	Daily Recommended Nutrition
Calories (kcal)	105	2000
Fat (g)	6	65
Saturated Fat (g)	1	20
Trans Fat (g)	0	
Poly Unsat Fat (g)	0.4	
Mono Unsat Fat (g)	4	
Cholesterol (mg)	0	300
Sodium (mg)	290	2400
Carbohydrates (g)	11	300
Dietary Fiber (g)	4	25
Total Sugars (g)	6	
Protein (g)	2	50
Vitamin A (IU)	0.5	5000
Vitamin C (mg)	60	91
Calcium (mg)	89	1000
Iron (mg)	1	18

Mustard Greens

Total Servings: 4
Serving Size: 1 cup

Growing up, I remember my mom cooking her greens with some sort of cured pork meat such as ham hocks or pig tails. Since changing my diet, I have removed these from my recipe and made other substitutions to bring out more of the natural flavors of the mustard greens.

2 cups water

2 pounds frozen mustard greens

¾ teaspoon Celtic Sea Salt® Brand

¼ teaspoon agave nectar syrup

¼ cup extra-virgin olive oil

¾ cup chopped onion

4½ teaspoons onion powder

½ teaspoon spicy vinegar, (see recipe, page 27) optional

Bring water to a rolling boil in a large saucepan; add all of the ingredients. Reduce heat to medium and simmer, covered, until the greens are tender, about 25 to 30 minutes. (The cook time will vary based on how tender you like your greens.) If desired, serve with spicy vinegar.

Tidbits

Fresh mustard greens can also be used with this recipe. Be sure to cut off the stems and remove any bugs or damaged leaves, and wash the leaves in cool water, at least twice. Stack several leaves and roll, tightly; cut the leaves into ¼-inch strips and cook as instructed above.

If not vegetarian, substitute 1 cup of the water with 1 cup of low sodium chicken broth or add ½ cup chopped, smoked turkey leg, for even more flavor.

Try this recipe with other greens such as turnips, kale, and chard. Depending on desired tenderness, you may have to adjust the cook time.

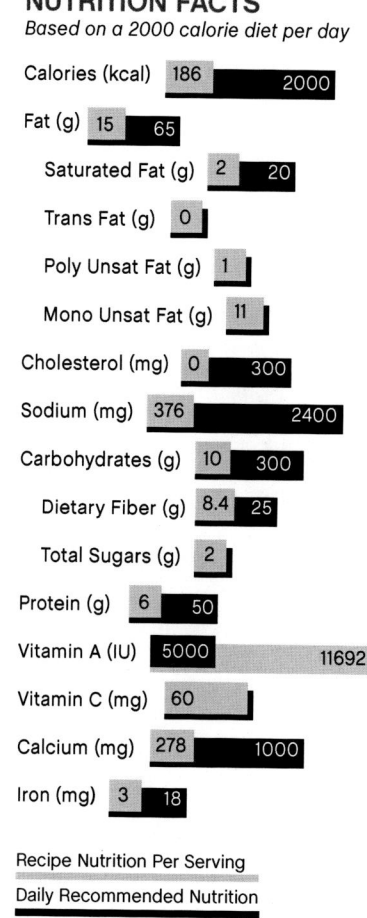

NUTRITION FACTS
Based on a 2000 calorie diet per day

Nutrient	Per Serving	Daily Recommended
Calories (kcal)	186	2000
Fat (g)	15	65
Saturated Fat (g)	2	20
Trans Fat (g)	0	
Poly Unsat Fat (g)	1	
Mono Unsat Fat (g)	11	
Cholesterol (mg)	0	300
Sodium (mg)	376	2400
Carbohydrates (g)	10	300
Dietary Fiber (g)	8.4	25
Total Sugars (g)	2	
Protein (g)	6	50
Vitamin A (IU)	5000	11692
Vitamin C (mg)	60	
Calcium (mg)	278	1000
Iron (mg)	3	18

Recipe Nutrition Per Serving

Daily Recommended Nutrition

Southern Style Green Beans

Total Servings: 6
Serving Size: ½ cup

This is an old time classic in my neck of the woods that mom cooked quite often. I remember having green beans whenever she cooked rice and gravy with fried chicken. Of course, I have taken this classic southern recipe and made it just as delicious but a lot healthier. If you never liked green beans, this dish will give you a different perspective; so give this version a try.

¼ cup extra-virgin olive oil

¾ cup chopped onion

1 medium clove garlic

1 pound frozen (or fresh) cut green beans

2½ cups water

½ teaspoon plus ⅛ teaspoon Celtic Sea Salt® Brand

Pinch ground black pepper

1 tablespoon onion powder

⅛ teaspoon garlic powder

1 tablespoon agave nectar syrup

Heat oil in a large saucepan, over medium heat about 1 to 2 minutes. Add onions and garlic and stir, continually about 1 to 2 minutes. Add beans, water, salt, pepper, onion powder, garlic powder, and syrup, and cook, covered, over medium heat about 1 to 1½ hours, or until desired tenderness. (There should be very little water in the pot.)

Tidbits

When using fresh green beans, pick out the speckled beans, rinse and dry. Trim the ends (about ¼-inch down from both ends) and cut beans into 2 to 3-inch long pieces. Add an additional cup of water and cook over medium heat for an extra 30 minutes.

To really give these green beans a Southern spin, add 6 small boiling potatoes (rinsed and halved) or 1 cup chopped turnip roots (washed and peeled) during the last 15 to 20 minutes of the cook time.

NUTRITION FACTS
Based on a 2000 calorie diet per day

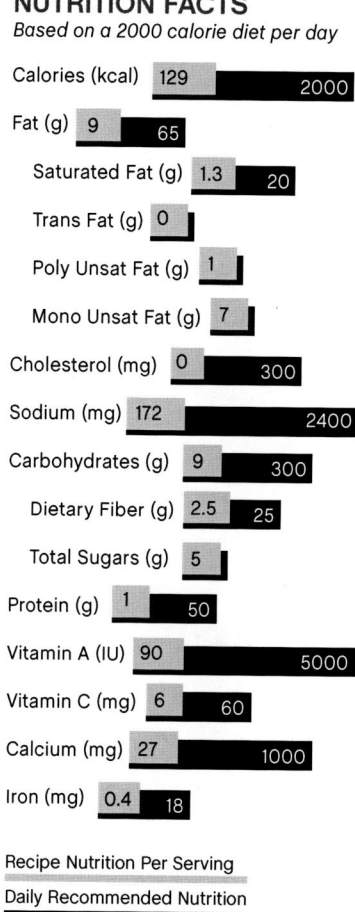

Nutrient	Per Serving	Daily Recommended
Calories (kcal)	129	2000
Fat (g)	9	65
Saturated Fat (g)	1.3	20
Trans Fat (g)	0	
Poly Unsat Fat (g)	1	
Mono Unsat Fat (g)	7	
Cholesterol (mg)	0	300
Sodium (mg)	172	2400
Carbohydrates (g)	9	300
Dietary Fiber (g)	2.5	25
Total Sugars (g)	5	
Protein (g)	1	50
Vitamin A (IU)	90	5000
Vitamin C (mg)	6	60
Calcium (mg)	27	1000
Iron (mg)	0.4	18

Recipe Nutrition Per Serving

Daily Recommended Nutrition

Candied Butternut Squash

Total Servings: 2
Serving Size: ½ cup

I didn't know what this funny looking squash was when I first saw it—it had a long neck, a round bottom and a hard exterior. After I figured out how to cook this bright orange delight, I was pleasantly surprised with the natural, sweet flavor of this winter squash. In fact, it reminded me of the sweet potato so I decided to prepare it in a similar way as my mother prepared candied yams. The cinnamon and syrup, makes this squash a delicious candied yam alternative!

1 pound butternut squash

4 teaspoons agave nectar syrup

¼ teaspoon cinnamon

Pinch ground cloves

1 Preheat the oven to 350°F. Peel butternut squash with a vegetable peeler and cut squash into ½-inch thick slices. Remove any seeds and strings with a spoon. Put squash onto a baking sheet lined with parchment paper (or aluminum foil) and bake about 40 to 50 minutes. Place the baking sheet on to a cooling rack; let cool about 5 to 8 minutes.

2 Add syrup, cinnamon, and cloves to a small saucepan and stir with a small spoon until well mixed. Simmer, uncovered over low heat 1 to 2 minutes; add butternut squash slices and coat with the syrup mixture.

Tidbit

For a savory vegetable side dish, replace the syrup, cinnamon and cloves with 1/2 teaspoon extra-virgin olive oil and 2 teaspoons chopped fresh or dried sage leaves. Bake, uncovered, for 40 to 50 minutes, or until desired tenderness.

NUTRITION FACTS
Based on a 2000 calorie diet per day

Nutrient	Per Serving	Daily Recommended
Calories (kcal)	82	2000
Fat (g)	0.1	65
Saturated Fat (g)	.02	20
Trans Fat (g)	0	
Poly Unsat Fat (g)	.04	
Mono Unsat Fat (g)	.01	
Cholesterol (mg)	0	300
Sodium (mg)	4	2400
Carbohydrates (g)	22	300
Dietary Fiber (g)	4	25
Total Sugars (g)	12	
Protein (g)	1	50
Vitamin A (IU)	5000	11435
Vitamin C (mg)	16	60
Calcium (mg)	46	1000
Iron (mg)	1	18

Recipe Nutrition Per Serving

Daily Recommended Nutrition

Cornless Cornbread Muffins

Total Servings: 12
Serving Size: 2 muffins

This recipe is a twist on momma's cornbread recipe. Unlike her recipe, this one substitutes the cornmeal with gluten-free millet flour. I developed this recipe after receiving a list of potential inflammatory foods that I should avoid, which included corn. Cornless cornbread muffins are great for those who battle with arthritis. Trust me, you won't miss the cornmeal!

2 tablespoons ground flaxseeds

6 tablespoons water

1 cup millet flour

1 cup Bob's Red Mill whole grain brown rice flour

4 teaspoons baking powder

⅛ teaspoon Celtic Sea Salt® Brand

¼ teaspoon plus ⅛ teaspoon guar gum

2 tablespoons agave nectar syrup

1¼ cups rice milk (or water)

¼ cup olive oil

1   Preheat the oven to 350°F. Whisk ground flaxseeds and water in a small bowl with a small wire whisk; let stand, about 2 to 3 minutes. The consistency should be similar to an egg that has been beaten.

2   Whisk millet flour, rice flour, baking powder, salt, guar gum, agave syrup, milk and oil in a large bowl with a large wire whisk. Stir in the flaxseed mixture and mix thoroughly until the batter is creamy and smooth; if too thick and difficult to stir, add an additional tablespoon of milk or water until the batter is easier to mix.

3   Pour the batter into a non-stick mini muffin pan, filling about three-fourths full; make sure that each section has equal amount of batter. Bake for 15 minutes, until the muffins are puffed and golden brown. If desired, use baking paper muffin cups for easy clean-up.

Tidbits

Any kind of bakeware can be used to bake these muffins, but the traditional pan that is most often used is the cast iron skillet. When using cast iron skillets, whether seasoned or unseasoned, coat with oil to prevent sticking.

If muffins are not golden brown on top, set the oven temperature to broil. Lightly brush the top of the muffins with about 1/4 teaspoon olive oil and place back into the oven on the top rack. Broil until the top of the muffins achieves desired golden brown color, about 1 or 1 1/2 minutes.

NUTRITION FACTS
Based on a 2000 calorie diet per day

	Per Serving	Daily Recommended
Calories (kcal)	142	2000
Fat (g)	6	65
Saturated Fat (g)	1	20
Trans Fat (g)	0	
Poly Unsat Fat (g)	0.3	
Mono Unsat Fat (g)	4	
Cholesterol (mg)	0	300
Sodium (mg)	200	2400
Carbohydrates (g)	20	300
Dietary Fiber (g)	2	25
Total Sugars (g)	3	
Protein (g)	2	50
Vitamin A (IU)	7	5000
Vitamin C (mg)	0	60
Calcium (mg)	18	1000
Iron (mg)	2	18

Recipe Nutrition Per Serving

Daily Recommended Nutrition

Black-Eyed Peas

Total Servings: 6
Serving Size: ½ cup

Black-eyed peas are a soul food tradition typically eaten for New Year's dinner to symbolize good luck and prosperity. Holding to that tradition, every year, my mom would cook her black-eyed peas, greens and cornbread! I love eating these beans, despite the time of year, because they are tasty and they cook in less time in comparison to other beans!

2 cups dried black-eyed peas

2 quarts water (8 cups)

1 cup chopped onion

1 teaspoon Celtic Sea Salt® Brand

3 tablespoons onion powder

½ teaspoon garlic powder

3 tablespoons extra-virgin olive oil

2 teaspoons agave nectar syrup

¼ teaspoons ground black pepper

½ cup chopped okra (optional)

1 Discard any peas that are speckled or rotten. Add dried peas to a large bowl filled with 4 cups of the water. Let the peas soak for 1 to 2 hours. Drain the peas and rinse.

2 Transfer peas to a medium pot and add the remaining 4 cups water. Bring peas to a rolling boil; add onion, sea salt, onion and garlic powders, olive oil, agave syrup and black pepper and cook, covered, over medium heat until creamy, about 2 hours. If desired, add okra during the last 15 minutes of the cook time.

Tidbits

Frozen black-eyed peas can be used. There is no need to soak; reduce cook time to about 1 to 1½ hours. You can also use this recipe with dried lentils instead of the black-eyed peas.

To cream the peas, slightly open the lid of the pot and bring peas to a rolling boil. Continue to let the peas boil until they become soft and creamy. This may take about 10 to 15 minutes.

NUTRITION FACTS
Based on a 2000 calorie diet per day

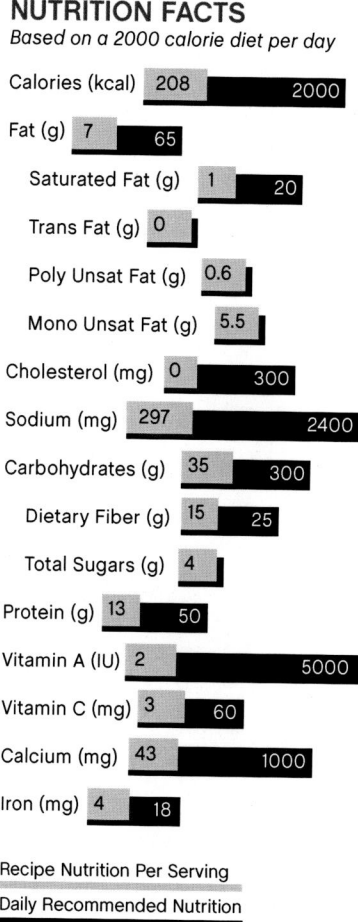

	Recipe Nutrition Per Serving	Daily Recommended Nutrition
Calories (kcal)	208	2000
Fat (g)	7	65
Saturated Fat (g)	1	20
Trans Fat (g)	0	
Poly Unsat Fat (g)	0.6	
Mono Unsat Fat (g)	5.5	
Cholesterol (mg)	0	300
Sodium (mg)	297	2400
Carbohydrates (g)	35	300
Dietary Fiber (g)	15	25
Total Sugars (g)	4	
Protein (g)	13	50
Vitamin A (IU)	2	5000
Vitamin C (mg)	3	60
Calcium (mg)	43	1000
Iron (mg)	4	18

Recipe Nutrition Per Serving

Daily Recommended Nutrition

Old Fashioned Lemonade

Total Servings: 6
Serving Size: 1 cup

This refreshing drink is an old time classic that needs no big introduction. Lemonade has always been a staple beverage in my house as a child. I remember those days of rolling lots of lemons trying to soften them before squeezing all of the juice into a bowl. I have upgraded from the days of rolling lemons, but I haven't replaced the love I have for this all-time classic, refreshing drink!

2½ large lemons, peeled and seeded (or ½ cup fresh lemon juice)

6¼ cups water

¾ cup plus 2 teaspoons agave nectar syrup

1   Process the peeled lemons in a juice extractor (juicer). Be sure to follow the manufacturer's instructions as indicated with your machine.

2   Add lemon juice, water and syrup to a large pitcher and stir. Serve chilled.

Tidbits

If you do not have a juicer, roll the lemons until they become soft. Halve lemons and squeeze until all juice has been extracted. (Additional lemons may be needed to obtain ½ cup juice.) Filter juice using a mesh strainer to remove seeds and pulp.

To make green tea lemonade, before adding the water to the juice, bring 4 cups of the water to a brisk boil. Pour the water over 6 tea bags in a large pitcher; let steep for 10 to 15 minutes. Remove the tea bags and mix tea with the lemon juice, syrup and the remaining 2½ cups water with a large spoon. Add additional syrup if needed.

NUTRITION FACTS
Based on a 2000 calorie diet per day

Nutrient	Recipe Per Serving	Daily Recommended
Calories (kcal)	132	2000
Fat (g)	0	65
Saturated Fat (g)	0	20
Trans Fat (g)	0	
Poly Unsat Fat (g)	0	
Mono Unsat Fat (g)	0	
Cholesterol (mg)	0	300
Sodium (mg)	0.2	2400
Carbohydrates (g)	36	300
Dietary Fiber (g)	2	25
Total Sugars (g)	32	
Protein (g)	0.1	50
Vitamin A (IU)	4	5000
Vitamin C (mg)	1	60
Calcium (mg)	9	1000
Iron (mg)	.01	18

Recipe Nutrition Per Serving

Daily Recommended Nutrition

Spicy Vinegar

Total Servings: 20
Serving Size: 1 tablespoon

Vinegar and peppers were a staple condiment in most restaurants in my hometown, and my mom and I used it frequently. We would pour this spicy vinegar over collard, mustard, or turnip greens prior to eating. This vinegar is so versatile and can also be used to make salad dressings or mixed in a stir-fry.

2 cups organic brown rice vinegar

15 whole Serrano peppers, rinsed and pat dry

2 cloves garlic, peeled and thinly sliced (optional)

1 Insert peppers into a clean bottle (about 16 ounces). If using garlic cloves, put inside the bottle after the peppers have been inserted.

2 Bring brown rice vinegar to a rolling boil in a small sauce pan; remove from heat and pour into the bottle using a funnel to prevent spillage. Close and let stand for at least a day before using.

Tidbits

The longer the vinegar sets, the more flavor is extracted from the peppers. This vinegar has a long shelf life and can be stored at room temperature.

Use any type of bottle; the recipe will change depending on the size. To measure the appropriate amount of vinegar needed, pour vinegar into the selected clean bottle prior to boiling.

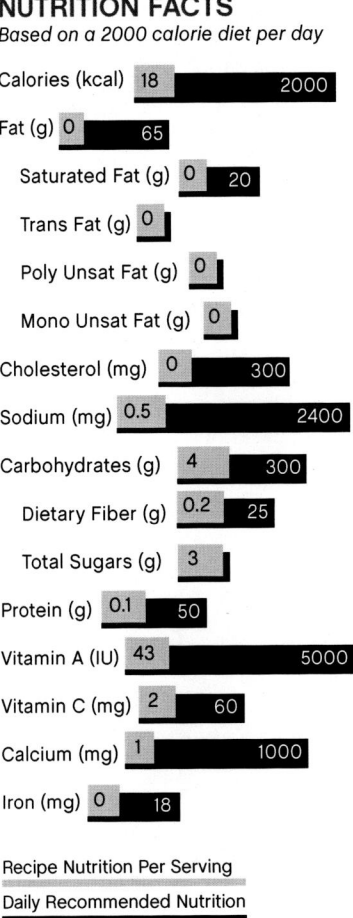

NUTRITION FACTS
Based on a 2000 calorie diet per day

	Recipe Nutrition Per Serving	Daily Recommended Nutrition
Calories (kcal)	18	2000
Fat (g)	0	65
Saturated Fat (g)	0	20
Trans Fat (g)	0	
Poly Unsat Fat (g)	0	
Mono Unsat Fat (g)	0	
Cholesterol (mg)	0	300
Sodium (mg)	0.5	2400
Carbohydrates (g)	4	300
Dietary Fiber (g)	0.2	25
Total Sugars (g)	3	
Protein (g)	0.1	50
Vitamin A (IU)	43	5000
Vitamin C (mg)	2	60
Calcium (mg)	1	1000
Iron (mg)	0	18

Recipe Nutrition Per Serving

Daily Recommended Nutrition

Gumbo

Total Servings: 8
Serving Size: 1 cup

I created this gumbo when I was craving some of my momma's gumbo, which I could no longer eat. Though this gumbo is not the real deal, it is a very close resemblance. This gumbo is a great substitute for people who cannot have shellfish or tomatoes. With the changes that I made with the original recipe, I was so shocked that my new creation was able to capture the essence of Louisiana gumbo. I think you will be pleasantly surprised with the flavor and texture—my mom was!

1½ pounds wild cod fillets, rinsed and cubed (bite-sized)

2 boneless, skinless chicken thighs, rinsed and cubed (optional)

2 quarts water

1 cup chopped green onions

1 cup chopped celery

¾ cup chopped yellow onions

2 tablespoons ground gumbo filé

1½ teaspoons Celtic Sea Salt® Brand

¼ teaspoon granulated garlic

2 tablespoons onion powder

¼ teaspoon red pepper flakes

⅛ teaspoon ground white pepper

2 cups chopped okra

¼ medium fresh beet, without top, rinsed and peeled

1 Add water, green onions, celery and yellow onions to a large pot and bring to a rolling boil. Stir in the gumbo filé, and cook, with the lid semi-covered, over medium heat, until the gumbo filé has dissolved, about 10 to 15 minutes. Add the sea salt, granulated garlic, onion powder, red pepper flakes, white pepper, and okra, stirring often until well mixed; simmer, covered for 15 to 20 minutes, or until the okra is cooked into smaller pieces. (Observe the gumbo mixture periodically to ensure that it does not boil over.)

2 Add the beet to the gumbo for color. (If desired, add cubed chicken during this step.) Reduce heat to medium low and cook, covered, for 3 to 5 minutes (the gumbo mixture will start to change to a maroon color.) Remove the beet once you are satisfied with the color. Stir in the fish and simmer, covered over low heat, until the fish is opaque throughout, about 5 to 8 minutes.

Tidbits

Typically Louisiana gumbo is a brownish red color, and in order to maintain a similar color, I add beet slices to facilitate the color change from green to the brownish-red. Do not leave the beet quarter in the gumbo too long. The longer it is left in the gumbo, the more maroon it will become.

To make the traditional Louisiana gumbo, add the following to this recipe: 1 tablespoon tomato paste (instead of beets), 1/8 teaspoon white pepper, 2 boneless, skinless, chopped chicken thighs, 1 cup diced turkey or chicken sausage, 1 cup deveined shrimp (instead of cod), and 1 cooked dungeon crab broken into pieces; these additions will surely make the gumbo pop!

NUTRITION FACTS
Based on a 2000 calorie diet per day

Nutrient	Per Serving	Daily Recommended
Calories (kcal)	91	2000
Fat (g)	1	65
Saturated Fat (g)	0.1	20
Trans Fat (g)	0	
Poly Unsat Fat (g)	0.3	
Mono Unsat Fat (g)	0.1	
Cholesterol (mg)	31	300
Sodium (mg)	382	2400
Carbohydrates (g)	4	300
Dietary Fiber (g)	2	25
Total Sugars (g)	1	
Protein (g)	16	50
Vitamin A (IU)	198	5000
Vitamin C (mg)	10	60
Calcium (mg)	40	1000
Iron (mg)	1	18

Recipe Nutrition Per Serving

Daily Recommended Nutrition

Cornless Cornbread Dressing

Total Servings: 5
Serving Size: ¾ cup

For many years, Thanksgiving dinner was uneventful because I could not eat corn, which is the staple ingredient in cornbread dressing. I later learned about whole grain millet flour and became interested in using it as a cornmeal substitute in my dressing recipe because the color and texture were very similar to cornmeal. So, after baking a few unsuccessful batches, I finally created the right recipe that mimics my mother's cornbread dressing, even she was impressed!

2 cups finely chopped green onions

2 cups finely chopped celery

¾ cup plus 6 tablespoons water

⅛ cup plus 3 tablespoons olive oil

2 tablespoons ground flaxseeds

1 cup millet flour

1 cup Bob's Red Mill whole grain brown rice flour

4 teaspoons baking powder

¼ teaspoon plus ⅛ teaspoon guar gum

2 tablespoons agave nectar syrup

¾ cup rice milk

2 teaspoons ground onion powder

⅛ teaspoon Celtic Sea Salt® Brand

1. Preheat the oven to 350°F. Bring 3/4 cup of the water to a boil in a medium saucepan and add onions, celery and 3 tablespoons of the olive oil; cover and cook over low heat about 40 to 45 minutes. Remove from heat and let cool for 20 minutes.

2. Whisk ground flaxseeds and the remaining 6 tablespoons water in a small bowl; let stand for 2 to 3 minutes. The consistency should be similar to an egg that has been beaten.

3. Combine millet flour, rice flour, baking powder, guar gum, agave syrup, rice milk, the remaining 1/8 cup olive oil, and flaxseed mixture in a large bowl. Stir in the cooked seasoning, onion powder and salt with a large spoon until creamy and smooth.

4. Pour batter into an 8 x 8 glass baking dish. Bake on 350°F for 60 to 70 minutes. Use a toothpick to test for doneness. If no crumbs appear on the toothpick, remove dressing from oven. Let cool on a wire rack for 3 to 5 minutes.

5. Break bread into small bite-size pieces with a large spoon in the baking dish; the bread should have a very moist texture. Place dish back into the oven and bake for 8 to 10 minutes. Let bread cool for 5 to 10 minutes before serving.

Tidbit
There are many recipe variations for cornbread dressing; some are made with ground sage, chopped apples, raisins, or seafood. Create your own and follow this recipe as directed; be careful not to add too much extra liquid without increasing the amount of dry ingredients. It will definitely make a difference in the texture of this recipe.

NUTRITION FACTS
Based on a 2000 calorie diet per day

Nutrient	Per Serving	Daily Recommended
Calories (kcal)	321	2000
Fat (g)	15	65
Saturated Fat (g)	2	20
Trans Fat (g)	0	
Poly Unsat Fat (g)	1	
Mono Unsat Fat (g)	9	
Cholesterol (mg)	0	300
Sodium (mg)	471	2400
Carbohydrates (g)	44	300
Dietary Fiber (g)	5	25
Total Sugars (g)	9	
Protein (g)	6	50
Vitamin A (IU)	2213	5000
Vitamin C (mg)	10	60
Calcium (mg)	131	1000
Iron (mg)	4	18

Recipe Nutrition Per Serving

Daily Recommended Nutrition

Pot Roast

Total Servings: 8
Serving Size: ½-inch thick slice

My momma's pot roast was alway delicious. Though she would use a few shortcuts to help her create that perfect flavor, it was good every time! This is definitely not my momma's recipe, but it is truly a close runner-up. The roast and gravy in this recipe is just as tender and mouth-watering as I remembered as a little girl.

2 pounds chuck roast, rinsed

¾ cup chopped onion

1 large clove garlic, minced

3½ tablepsoons onion powder

1¾ teaspoons garlic powder

¼ teaspoon thyme leaves

¼ teaspoon chopped rosemary leaves

1¼ teaspoons Celtic Sea Salt® Brand

2½ cups water

2 tablespoons olive oil

3 tablespoons tapioca flour

1 tablespoon gluten free, all-purpose flour

1 medium bay leaf

1   Add ½ cup of the onions, garlic, onion powder, garlic powder, thyme, rosemary, salt and 2 cups of the water to a 5-quart oval slow cooker.

2   Mix the remaining ½ cup water and the tapioca flour with a wire whisk in a small bowl; add tapioca mixture to the slow cooker, stirring continually, until well mixed. Place the roast into the slow cooker and cook, covered, over high heat, until the meat is fork-tender, and easy to separate with a fork, about 4 hours. Reduce heat to low/warm, and simmer, covered, until gravy is prepared, about 30 minutes.

3   Preheat oil in a wide, large saucepan over medium-high heat; add the remaining chopped onions and cook, stirring continually, until onions start to turn slightly brown, about 1 or 2 minutes. Reduce heat to medium and add flour, stirring often until flour becomes a caramel or golden brown color, with no flour lumps, about 3 to 4 minutes. (This will become the base for the gravy.) Whisk in 3 cups of the pot roast broth, slowly, stirring constantly, until the flour mixture (also known as roux) is well combined and smooth. Add bay leaf and pot roast to the gravy and simmer, covered, stirring occasionally, about 10 to 15 minutes.

Tidbit

The required cook time is dependent on the slow cooker brand type. Some brands cook foods really fast and others cook relatively slow, so you may need to adjust the cook time. Review your slow cooker manual prior to startingv.

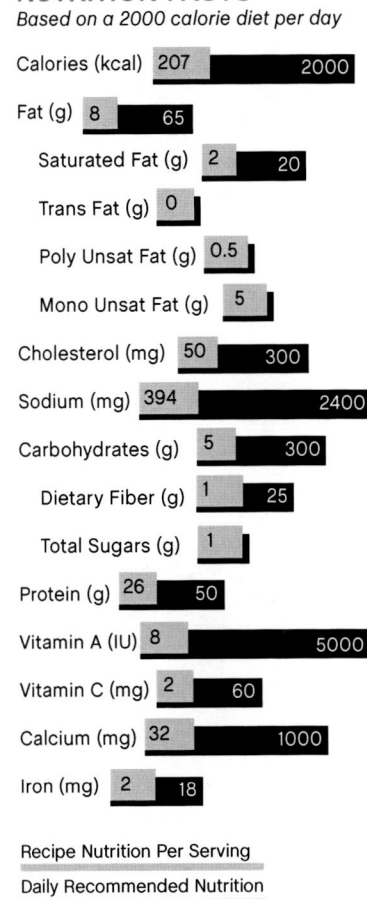

NUTRITION FACTS
Based on a 2000 calorie diet per day

Calories (kcal)	207	2000
Fat (g)	8	65
Saturated Fat (g)	2	20
Trans Fat (g)	0	
Poly Unsat Fat (g)	0.5	
Mono Unsat Fat (g)	5	
Cholesterol (mg)	50	300
Sodium (mg)	394	2400
Carbohydrates (g)	5	300
Dietary Fiber (g)	1	25
Total Sugars (g)	1	
Protein (g)	26	50
Vitamin A (IU)	8	5000
Vitamin C (mg)	2	60
Calcium (mg)	32	1000
Iron (mg)	2	18

Recipe Nutrition Per Serving

Daily Recommended Nutrition

Brown Rice

Total Servings: 2
Serving Size: ½ cup

Brown rice definitely took a lot of mental preparation in order for me to give up white rice! However, once I learned that the healthy nutrients have been stripped away from the natural brown rice and polished white, I knew that I had to learn to eat brown rice. It took a few tries for me to cook perfect brown rice—it was either too hard or mushy. But after lots of trial and error, I finally got the right method. So, if you had similar experiences of under cooking or over cooking brown rice, don't give up; instead try this recipe—it works every time!

½ cup uncooked long-grain brown rice

½ cup water

¼ teaspoon Celtic Sea Salt® Brand (optional)

¼ teaspoon turmeric (optional)

1. Place the rice in a fine mesh strainer set over a bowl. Rinse under running water, swishing rice with hands. Drain thoroughly. Continue until the water is clear, no longer brown.

2. Add rice and water to a small saucepan and bring to a boil over high heat. (If using salt and turmeric, add during this step.) Reduce heat to low; cook, covered until the rice is tender and the water is fully absorbed, about 50 to 60 minutes. Let stand, covered, about 5 minutes to 10 minutes. With a fork, gently lift the rice to fluff before serving.

Tidbits

The key tip for cooking perfect rice, is to make sure that you use equal parts water and rice—i.e. 2 cups water and 2 cups rice. If you want the rice a little stickier/softer, then just add more water. This recipe will work for other varieties of whole grain rice.

Brown rice is a whole grain and is more nutritious than the highly refined white rice. Unlike the natural brown rice, white rice has been processed with the outer layers (the bran and germ) of the whole grain removed.

NUTRITION FACTS
Based on a 2000 calorie diet per day

Nutrient	Per Serving	Daily Recommended
Calories (kcal)	108	2000
Fat (g)	1	65
Saturated Fat (g)	0.2	20
Trans Fat (g)	0	
Poly Unsat Fat (g)	0.3	
Mono Unsat Fat (g)	0.3	
Cholesterol (mg)	0	300
Sodium (mg)	5	2400
Carbohydrates (g)	22	300
Dietary Fiber (g)	2	25
Total Sugars (g)	0.3	
Protein (g)	3	50
Vitamin A (IU)	0	5000
Vitamin C (mg)	0	60
Calcium (mg)	10	1000
Iron (mg)	0.4	18

Recipe Nutrition Per Serving

Daily Recommended Nutrition

Whole Roasted Chicken

Total Servings: 8
Serving Size: 1 piece

Sometimes you don't want to be bothered with preparing and cooking a 10 pound turkey to pair with the cornless cornbread dressing. Then do not fret, instead, just use a 3.5 pound whole broiler chicken or hen. It will be less space in the fridge, less prep time, and less cook time!

3½ pounds broiler/fryer whole chicken, cleaned (inner chamber) and rinsed

1½ teaspoons garlic powder

1 tablespoon onion powder

1½ teaspoons Celtic Sea Salt® Brand

1½ teaspoon paprika

1 tablespoon ground black pepper

1½ teaspoons poultry seasoning

2 tablespoons plus 1 teaspoon olive oil

1. Position the oven rack in the center of the oven. Preheat the oven to 350 degrees. Grease the rack of a roasting pan with 1 tablespoon of the olive oil using a basting brush (or use a baking sheet with a greased cooling rack placed on top of the pan); this will allow the chicken drippings to fall to the bottom of the pan. Line the bottom with aluminum foil for easy clean-up.

2. Combine the garlic powder, onion powder, salt, paprika, black pepper and poultry seasoning in a small bowl; reserve ½ teaspoon. Mix the reserved ½ teaspoon of the dry seasoning mixture with 1 tablespoon of the olive oil in a cup with a wire whisk. Fill an injector with the olive oil seasoning mixture. Remove the neck, giblets and organs from the whole chicken; rinse thoroughly with running water. Fold chicken wing tips underneath the drum portion (the biggest part of the wing); this will form a triangle shape. Place the whole chicken into a large bowl. Inject the seasoning into various parts of the chicken, especially the breast.

3. Use fingers to loosen the skin of the chicken that covers the breast by sliding your fingers between the skin and the flesh, taking care not to tear the skin. Season with the remaining seasoning mixture inside the pocket defined by each breast half, thigh and the inner cavity of the chicken. Then season the outside of the chicken with the remaining seasoning. Immediately, rinse hands in warm, soapy water

4. Place on the chicken so that it sits back side up onto the greased roaster rack. Bake for 1 hour 30 minutes. Remove from the oven. Turn the chicken and position it so that it sits stomach side up. Baste with the remaining 1 teaspoon of the olive using a pastry brush. Place back in the oven and roast for another 15 minutes or until an instant-read thermometer inserted into the thickest part of the breast away from the bone registers 160 degrees.

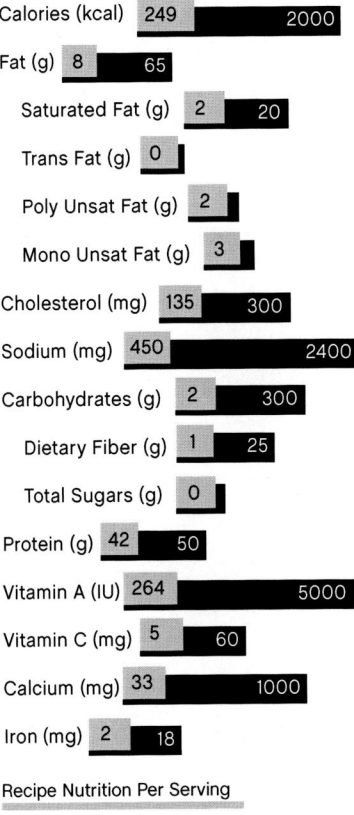

NUTRITION FACTS
Based on a 2000 calorie diet per day

(Single serving without skin)

	Recipe	Daily
Calories (kcal)	249	2000
Fat (g)	8	65
Saturated Fat (g)	2	20
Trans Fat (g)	0	
Poly Unsat Fat (g)	2	
Mono Unsat Fat (g)	3	
Cholesterol (mg)	135	300
Sodium (mg)	450	2400
Carbohydrates (g)	2	300
Dietary Fiber (g)	1	25
Total Sugars (g)	0	
Protein (g)	42	50
Vitamin A (IU)	264	5000
Vitamin C (mg)	5	60
Calcium (mg)	33	1000
Iron (mg)	2	18

Recipe Nutrition Per Serving

Daily Recommended Nutrition

Apples á la Mode

Total Servings: 2
Serving Size: ½ cup

I love apple pie á la mode and anything else served á la mode style—simply put, I love anything served with ice cream! Since removing wheat from my diet, I struggled to find desserts, so after craving apple pie, I decided to make my version of a no-crust apple pie á la mode that's not only yummy, but also low in calories. If you love apple pie á la mode, then you have to try this recipe.

2 medium gala apples, rinsed and peeled

¼ teaspoon cinnamon

⅛ teaspoon nutmeg

⅛ teaspoon ground cloves

⅛ teaspoon stevia

1 tablespoon agave nectar syrup

3 tablespoons water

1 scoop non-dairy ice cream (about ½ cup)

1   Cut apples into quarters and remove the stem and core; chop apples into small cubes.

2   Add apples, cinnamon, nutmeg, cloves, stevia, agave syrup, and water to a small saucepan and cook, covered, over medium heat, until the apples are tender (soft), about 40 to 45 minutes. Use a fork to pierce the apples to determine if the apples are at the desired tenderness. Be sure that the apples are not too soft then it will become applesauce. Serve apples in a bowl or martini glass, topped with ice cream.

Tidbits

The type of apples used in this recipe is important because of the different levels of sweetness. In my opinion, Fuji and gala are two of the sweetest apples. If you like very sweet desserts, add an extra tablespoon of syrup.

This recipe is versatile and can be used with other fruits such as pears, peaches and figs!

NUTRITION FACTS
Based on a 2000 calorie diet per day

Nutrient	Per Serving	Daily Recommended
Calories (kcal)	201	2000
Fat (g)	3	65
Saturated Fat (g)	0.3	20
Trans Fat (g)	0	
Poly Unsat Fat (g)	0.1	
Mono Unsat Fat (g)	.01	
Cholesterol (mg)	0	300
Sodium (mg)	52	2400
Carbohydrates (g)	45	300
Dietary Fiber (g)	6	25
Total Sugars (g)	35	
Protein (g)	0.5	50
Vitamin A (IU)	149	5000
Vitamin C (mg)	9	60
Calcium (mg)	24	1000
Iron (mg)	1	18

Recipe Nutrition Per Serving

Daily Recommended Nutrition

Glossary

This glossary includes a brief definition or description of key food and health vocabularies that were used throughout this cookbook.

Agave nectar syrup – Agave nectar syrup is a sweetener that comes from the blue agave cactus plant.

Celtic Sea Salt® Brand – Celtic Sea Salt® Brand is authentic, unprocessed sea salt that is free of pesticides, anti-caking or bleaching agents and is hand-harvested in France.

Gumbo Filé – Gumbo Filé, also called filé powder, is a spice made from dried and ground sassafras leaves. It is used sparingly in gumbo as thickening agent, giving it a distinctive flavor and texture.

Flaxseeds – Flaxseeds contain high levels Omega-3 fatty acids, which may benefit the heart. Flaxseeds have a slight nutty flavor and range from deep amber to reddish brown color depending upon whether the flax is of the golden or brown variety.

Food allergy – Food allergies occur when the immune system rejects food, causing reactions such as throat swelling, cramps or severe and life-threatening conditions. These immune system reactions can occur immediately when the food is ingested or at a later time (about 1 to 3 days) after the food has been ingested.

Food intolerance – Food intolerance is the inability to properly digest or process certain foods. Food intolerances do not impact the immune system but usually triggers a digestive reaction.

Gluten – Gluten is the mixture of proteins found in wheat grains such as rye, wheat and barley. Gluten gives wheat dough its elastic texture.

Guar gum – Guar gum, a natural gum, is an edible thickening agent extracted from the guar bean.

Millet flour – Millet is a grain that has been in existence for many centuries and is widely produced around the world—India and Africa are the top producers. Millet does not contain gluten, but has a similar protein profile as wheat.

Quinoa – Quinoa is a 6000 year old seed that originated out of the Andes Mountain of South America. Quinoa is not a grain though it is cooked and eaten as a grain. It has the most protein than any other grain and it is a complete protein containing all nine essential amino acids that the body needs.

Stevia – Stevia is made from the plant rebaudiana and claims to have up to 300 times the sweetness of sugar. It has no calories and no glycemic index; it is all natural and does not contain acetic acid, formaldehyde, chloride, etc.

Stay connected with Rhonda by visiting the website: www.rhondascooking.com.
You can also follow Rhonda on:
www.twitter.com/rhondascooking
www.facebook.com/SoWhatCanIEatNow
www.intstagram.com/RhondasCooking

If you have any questions concerning these recipes or any products used in
these recipes, email info@rhondascooking.com or write to the following address:

PO Box 153, Laveen, AZ 85339

www.rhondascooking.com

Index

Made in the USA
Coppell, TX
20 October 2021

64339179R10029